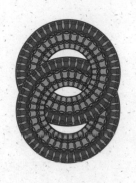

So Close

✕✕

So Close

POEMS

Peggy Penn

CavanKerry ❖ Press LTD.

FORT LEE, NEW JERSEY

Library of Congress Cataloging-in-Publication Data

Penn, Peggy, 1931–
    So close / Peggy Penn.
        p.   cm.
    ISBN 0-9678856-4-7
    I. Title.
PS3566.E475 S6 2001
811'.6—dc21   00-052358

Cover painting: François Clouet, *La carta amorosa*, c. 1570.
Oil on paper on panel, 41,4 x 55 cm,
© Museo Thyssen-Bornemisza, Madrid.

Cover and text design by Charles Casey Martin

FIRST EDITION

*T*his book is dedicated to my clan in order of their appearance:

Arthur

Matthew, Molly, Yann, Candace, Ethan, Dylan, Liam, and Aidan

Table of Contents

⨉⨉

THREE

FOUR

Foreword

✕✕

Calling a book of poems *So Close* insists on intimacy in our age of irony. In Peggy Penn's work, people, ideas, and metaphors all come so close to one another that gaps are closed, cool distances become warm, and the world achieves an easeful rapport. In Penn's realms, earthiness combines with delicacy, intellectual and social ideas unite with physical and sexual play, health enters the castle of sickness, age roams childhood, and the purity of childhood passions infuses all adult experiences. For this poet a tête-à-tête between two beings—even between two states of being—becomes an ars poetica.

To introduce a poet's first book is usually to explain a kind of emerging essence that will flower later on. But this book already is a flower. Not only are certain poems like "Hyacinth," "Postcard," or "L'arrangement: Paris" full of floral images, but even when a flower is nowhere in sight one has the sense that the whole book is in bloom. Penn's poems define growth, not as a culmination, but as a process of culminating: flowering is formed by a lifetime of experience. Penn's voice, both fresh and mature, demonstrates the linguistic growth we experience as we use language both again and anew.

For some of us, language becomes increasingly supple the longer we use it, just as our observations become increasingly daring the longer we live. Penn seems to have perfectly warmed her verbal legs, now always ready to dance. Whether the speaker disports with a bear who "shits enough to fill a hubcap" in "Dancing in the Dark" or a couple waltzes on the margins of mental illness in "Their Hippocampus Stomp"; whether the World War II veterans shuffle off to Buffalo in "Vets" or dancing is merely suggested—as in the poem "Phantoms" which opens, "I've been carrying / my leg for some time now"—the movement of the body through space always implies a movement through time.

And these two dimensions in Penn's work don't always have an exact overlay. Space and time coexist in a marriage that accommodates the two partners' personalities—for in her poems all natural life has personality, whether a hibiscus or a turtle or a sedge in a pond, and, likewise, all manner of time has personality, since we tell time in Penn's world by the stages of growth, whether at the end of life when a bottle of Mylanta becomes "a turquoise angel" or at its beginnings when an infant, "quiet as a melon...flaunt[s] a raspberry navel." While solidly in this world, the poems have a whiff of the surreal, not so much in their images as in how these images point to a perception of how life is lived. The imaginary bear actually shits. The turquoise plastic Mylanta bottle actually is an angel—even while it is also a stomach soother. The inner and the outer, what is mentally processed or physically digested, have interrelationships that underpaint one another. While we can easily extricate these relationships using ordinary categories of body and soul, mental and physical, real and imagined, present and remembered, young and old, human and animal, pain and joy, Penn reminds us that the thoroughly lived life never enacts these binary categories.

Not that Penn blurs them—as an actor might blur herself into a character; rather, she chooses to acknowledge their daily, non-contradictory coexistence. Thus the poems aren't dreamlike, they are merely host to the many simultaneous levels of perception we all routinely experience but write about separately. Penn started adult life as an actor, and through that art found her vocation as a family therapist. As an internationally recognized family therapist who has fearlessly stepped into arenas of violence and illness, and who has worked writing into her interactions with patients, Penn is adept at asking the unaddressed question that will unlock love, releasing it into the network of a painfully frozen family group. Essentially, *So Close* is about love released from pain, sometimes as a genii, sometimes as a vapor, sometimes as a whole individual him- or herself.

Nowhere is her comfort with the coexistence of joy and pain so evident as in her love poems and in her humor. "Flies are the real nosologists," she says in "Ordinarily Your Nose," a funny, sexy poem about married love. Who writes about married love, anyway? What is there to say? Plenty, Penn knows, and she unfolds a folio of testaments to sexuality and mutual understanding. In her subjects she is an American naturalist, growing out of Dickinson, Moore, Bishop, Frost, and Williams, yet she always brings the natural emblem toward a psychological interaction. In the poem "Everything Comes," she quotes her husband's response to the anxiousness and frustration inside her desire to dig a pond, a home to myriad forms of life. "Everything comes to a pond," he says, and so his casual statement is borne out over years, as in fact whole generations—a family ecosystem—come to that pond.

Time inverts our self-definitions. Bodily closeness seems subverted when a doctor declares, "no intimacies for now." So distance plays a role in this book, especially as a surrender of the physical creates room for sacred, spiritual, and social intercourse. Because of the warmth of her voice, the liquidity of her memory, and her prosodic savoir faire, Peggy Penn's lines themselves form—and act like—a pond. She lures all emotions to her poems, to thrive in the presence of syllabic magic and frank human utterance.

Thus wisdom seems to flourish in this poetry, which holds all its disparate impulses so close.

—*Molly Peacock*

xi

One

Dancing in the Dark

for Nancy Goldberger

Tin cans rolling across the patio
wake me. Creeping downstairs I make a plan—
fling open the door to scare the raccoons
when a piece of the darkness separates
itself into a blurry massive shape:
on my lawn there is a bear! *a bear!*
Saliva all over the patio
where he's drooled and strewn four days of garbage.
Striped by moonlight, I watch his snout thrust deep
inside half-grapefruit rinds. He sneezes,

crams his dripping tongue inside a herring jar,
lumbers toward the compost heap and tossing
the matchstick fence over his shoulder
sits on top of the heap: bear so hungry...
moonlight caught on crystal tips of fur.
I reach for the phone, *they will shoot him....*
Rearing, he stands upright, swaggers
to the ash tree, beefy haunches plie
up and down, loosening his back in a long rub.
Once his ass is scratched, his penis drops

inches till he pisses, glaring—it lasts
minutes. I abandon the phone and my hand
floats spellbound like an oar on the air.
Between the pointed teeth in wet black gums
saliva rolls down his chest, and I feel
beads of my own sweat moving uncertainly,
finally looping under my right breast.

Reeling back to the patio he begins
a dance among the cans, a clattering,
paddling, sashay step! He turns, head up,

and through a confetti of moonlight I hear,
Dancing in the Dark. Beneath a mirrored ball
I dance back, swaying to his brush-step swing,
following his feet, just two on a floe,
a hoodlum freedom in my head, rocking
and stomping, bear on the patio, me
in the kitchen, his secret partner, turning
when he turns, lifting my bosom to him . . .
kicking my silent cans. But suddenly
he stops, drops down, lurches near my window

as though looking for something lost: a glove,
a dance card? Instead he finds the right spot
and shits enough to fill a hubcap, scuffs
to the edge of the dark and disappears.
Outside now, I stand in the smell, the lure
of rotten cantaloupe and mango skins
mixed with his steamy sulfurous sweat.
Forbidden Fruit hangs in the air; love
must be somewhere. I go back up the stairs
and put a blue hibiscus in my hair.

Open

The female beetle slits the mimosa branch,
fills it with eggs, it drops off, the beetles
hatch and the tree is pruned. A collabor-
ative act, so attuned, and not closing.

><

Women are never quite closed—notice—
handbags are often grasped but not snapped closed
inviting nosings round the opening.
It's a state of mind that makes room for arrivals

><

and more—we need not even guess at. Women
also dress that way: intuiting slits
buttons and snaps, shifts and wraps, and garter belts—
holding up half of nothing—frame an opening.

><

Oh the inlets and coves of women's clothes:
tides and moons pull bare arms out of armholes,
many-eyed frog closures on a light jacket,
let the mind hum a duet to a long-

><

sleeved tunic wandering past bushes,
brushing past drawstring pants to a sarong
on a perfumed, midriff river where
the lazy slit of her skirt drops back near the bank.

><

The Madonna del Parto for centuries
has enjoyed fame for her slit skirt,
parted to accept the annunciation.
Two angels pull back the rose curtains

><

advertising her holy, common state.
Even women's language is unfastened—
open like a suitcase—which if you unpacked—
you'd find enough long syllables for

><

the formal stretches and certainly short *e*'s
for daytime sports, culottes of vowels,
run-ons for aerobics, and alchemic puns
for the fast change, post-time woman.

><

Like the Madonna, I advertise,
confessing in every word that I dress
toward the guess of your glance. Hurrying
past the blet in the peach, I am trying
and trying on the ones that fit you.

Polity

for Arthur

I have a position that answers
each change in your position.
Excitor, your forearm bone
bows my hip, and hoping to safecrack
my dream, you prick my scheme,
then spoon me from behind
till we sit lying in our frog dialogue.
To my co-opting plea of knees
your forensic elbow replies,
I will, I do, Oh, take my side!

Thus point on counterpoint
do we anoint our various regions
and take, God knows, what polls
in sweet debate of nightly sleep.

Weight up on elbow,
one listens, sleeping,
while the other pees in the dark;
a hiss through serpentine sleep:
and then by accident you're back—
kissing me and climbing like a wild
white rose—and bending down,
your shadow protects me from eclipse.

Gentle night genital,
campfire where I warm my hands,
lets love smother argument.
Promise me you'll stay

until the reverent dawn pours down the day,
I petition, stay with me,
and we will be positioned
in our polity of love.

The Soup

On the day of your scan I make a soup
to wean us from meat. Beans soak and blanch
an hour while I slit open the cell-
ophane wrap on the celery, chopping
the ribs into small pieces, the size
of the stones that follow an avalanche.
Carrots sliced into see-through orange mem-
branes, others hacked into jagged boulders, bi-
sected as though by the pressure of shift-
ing plates. Onions at knife point, suppurate
and toss themselves into the hot oil. What
is left? two blind see-no-evil potatoes.
Sweet herbs: I pull apart ovate leaves
of basil and sweet marjoram. Red kidney
beans slip out of their bladder skins, rubbing
against the Great Limas. Together,
they give off a kind of scum which keeps down
the foaming boil; instead it heaves and
swells, trembling like a bosom but does not
spill out. Thank God for scum! *I rinse my knife,*
watching its gleaming edge rotate under
the water; now there is only the wait.

Gaps

The long gap between winter and spring
pretends ambivalence, the pleasure
of being of two minds. Walking, dazed, we glance off
each other, sinking into brown burlap ground;
coal-age sludge we can't get through. Anything new—
reeds for instance, so inclined, cripple
in its thickness. Varicose roots hold
across bare rock; cold to the touch as my hand.
Shoulders of willows shudder their pale leaves
as rain releases the deep winter wrinkles
gained in the long time you have been gone.

A dim sequelae of spring spreads out
in faded attic colors. Above us,
a gray plastic bag flaps in high branches;
torn banner, it lasted out the bitter winter.
The tapestry tree, always chivalrous,
with luteous needles soft as baby nails,
shades us from a sword of sun cutting through.
Predaceous bugs crawl warmly over your hand
toward the pond—leaving a watery message
too quick to read. . . . you gather our scattered words,
like small blue eggs, lay them on my tongue
and spring, apologetically, comes.

Torment

Grabbing her foot he throws her against the wall—
bangs her head on the floor, smashes
her in the belly with his fists. Thank God
she's made of rag and yarn—because the harms
are slight, except for one eye hanging
down...a loose blue thread, and on her butt
the yarn is broken, red. I can tell
the doll adores the passion of it all—
he, throwing her limb from limb, and she,
sprawling in limp wrecks of new positions.
And how fast her heart is beating...how
she thinks of him under the furniture;
all the dark afternoons; his touch stays
so tender, mysterious and blue.

Zona Viva

Mexico City Market

Something about the day of the night-before-leaving
teases the yellow smog into a dream light;
I walk in a gaslit dusk, breathless,
through the Zona Viva, to find a souvenir.
Now, almost disappeared beneath the shops
that sell their artifacts, sit soft mounds
of Indian women, working in their office
of children and rags. Whirling children,
tied by invisible strings, are learning
the subtracted gravity of the Zona Viva:
the strings cannot rappel them over the fell
of poverty's edge. They are hostage tops,
caught in the hands of their holders, blurring
in an exudation of women and myrrh.

Within the flags of paper lace, cut-out fish,
birds and braided dolls, a woman weaves in a strand
from her own shawl, not distinguishing
person from place. Watching me,
she opens her flower hand stirring
the sleeping baby in her skirt: begging,
her dropped petal fingers curl toward me,
arrowhead eyes fly toward me as I reach down
with a coin for her hand. In the gaping yellow night,
I feel my own child's hand pull me down.
"Am I going to die?" she asks, nearly grown,
I count to twenty.

Paris. An ovarian cyst after midnight
twists her to the floor; she is yours,
and mortal, avoid the hospital.
We lock in two curves, her back against my front,
between my knees, rocking, counting,
our breaths timed with her pain . . .
twenty seconds, and we rest in between . . .
helplessly, I am chanting, *"in - be - tween,*
. . . there is a small space between the pains
where we rest . . ." wet as seals, our holds slip,
counting, the small space comes,
we rest in long breaths.

"Ma, am I going to die?"
"Not while we breathe, no one dies . . .
count, it is time to count!"
We count again to twenty . . . and the hours slip,
even, now subsiding, you fall to my side.
I pull the sheet down to cover you,
my long lovely daughter, sleep in this bough
of arms and legs, while we wait
for some act of reinstatement,
until the fever breaks,
or the ancients return to the Zona Viva.

The Indian woman's eyes never leave my face
as I kneel down to her baby.
I buy a painted tin votive,
thanking God for a miracle. Permissibly,
we gaze at each other's hammock bodies,
listening to the script of origins,

seeing volcanoes overturn or spare the pyramids,
begin the tops or stop their orbital spin.
Inhale, suppose there is spirea in the air,
where the women sit, twilit, watching the day close,
a book held fast in the hand of a sleeper,
where it is written: in this place of accidents,
we are innocent. Inhale.

Hurricane

I ask, "What are you thinking of these days?"
moving through the August days of golden-
rod in our flawless, almost spent summer.
"Mortality..." you say. Suddenly,
the skin of life is burning and sticking
to our fingers. Springs and pins fly every-
where; the tools of animation, dis-
assembling. With outstretched war-bonnet wings,
the osprey lands on his nest to feed
his children; they snap the flapping fish
and fly off as he watches from his nest
of unrelinquished wishes. We nearly
step on a large mud turtle, driven over,
squeezed and cracked like chutney flavoring
the ground. Looking at you, I see a small
tug after the recent hurricane, pull
a foundering sub out of the sound.

Off White

My mother died last night. Illness distended
her size so that no clothes fit. The blinding
diamonds she loved must be left behind.

I buy her a white dress trimmed with crystal
beads. The saleslady smiles, *"Oh, she'll surely
like this, she'll need it for winter!"*

"Oh winter," I smile back, *"Yes, winter..."*
she shakes my outstretched hand; I look her
straight in the eye; my mother taught me that.

Inamorata Immaculata.
As martyrs can, she dies on a day
of even length, her chosen equinox,

in mid-September and I am forty.
She raises her body and screams, *"Help me
breathe!"* I try to rouse my father; (snoring,

waiting for her to die) to connect
her second oxygen tank. I am shouting,
"Let me do it!" *"NO!"* he shouts back, awake,

"Who do you think's running this God damn show!"
She closes her eyes to our familiar talk
and dying, runs out of air like a balloon.

Death seems to relax her. A small smile
appears on her face and she looks peaceful,
saintly, home. While my face, askew, retains

her final living grimace. The same
gaping mouth I had at nine when I viewed
my grandmother laid out in a pine box,

dun colored, like the plums in our cellar.
Horrified, my obese aunt throws herself
into the coffin, picks up her stiff

little mother as though to hurl her
all the way back to life. Flesh trembling
she howls, *"Ma! Oh Ma! Don't leave your girl. . . ."*

Staggering, they both crash to the floor
covered with the heads of flowers, stems
zigzagged and pointing, like the arrows in

Saint Sebastian. Appalled, my mother
turns my face to the wall, but I remember
the color of death—like the dried blood

on the arrows. I close my eyes to see
her face white and slightly
lilac; a place where blood has been.

Deceit

Lawless autumn, it rains without mercy—
as though lust for rot bows the big white heads
of phlox. Waiting in the yellow light
after the rain, I watch a pair of hawks drift,
following their prey. It is a prophet's light
sweeping the hills; something is coming.

Delphiniums, my population
of steady summer faces, torch the garden
in their last, pilot-blue light. Shadows
ink the water. Motionless, I hear the fish,
soft noise of coy scouting the spillway.
I am not deceived, the time of desiccation

has begun; the garden shows signs of rust.
I work against the rot and ruin; under the
asters my hands become loam, wide home of earth
with roses growing out my chest and sides
of silvering artemesia. I hear
the ring of foxglove bells that tolled my

warring father down in his English
foxhole hells . . . here in my garden I feel
the pardon he did not have. I dig in fear,
lest my hand find some old bone of mine
or other: I scramble like the mole, hidden
against the day I'm forbidden here.

On my sitting rock there's evidence
of a bird's evisceration; easy
brutality, the insurance of
existence, making room so we don't
miss it. My hand encloses the star-shaped
weeds but even pulling hard, I can't let go.

Is this how it will end? a slowly
closing darkness—then, winter
will descend, white with fear. . . .

Two

Calendar

April: The Voyage

Marginally home, the room is devoid
of any event except leaving.
*"How did your tattoo go, did you ask
for a rose?"* She opens her shirt to show me
her breasts, *"Not bad,"* she says, *"for 76?"*
"Beautiful," I agree. A radiation
zone scatters across her nude breast dunes,
as though she'd failed to make it through barbed wire.

May: Stories

Stories tell she was fragrant as the white
datura night bloomers she paints.

June: The Longest Days

Sitting on the sink is the turquoise angel,
Mylanta; powder still circling the rim
from a recent gulp. Two wet washrags hang
over the sink's yellow side, waiting for
mouth patrol. The chrome spout arches high
over the bowl; she must move it aside
when she gags.

Hope

A red amaryllis leans in her window,
no trumpets now but silky, sticky
blossoms still cling to my hand.

June: The Umbilical Lyre

We sink together into the time of her
childhood and the memories slip out like
afterbirth . . . sixteen, playing a Zenith
radio . . . too thin, dancing alone in
her badly fitted dress . . . her mother spies her,
"Who do you think you are?" "Gall," she says,
was in her mouth. *"Mama, I'm not doing well
here, let me leave, I have to leave, I'll do
better, you'll check me every week, you'll see."*
Home was an emptying place.

Umbilical Song

Her language becomes milky, tongue licking
the corners of her mouth into a smile
when she describes her daughter, and the cud
of grassy love words repeat themselves.

July: The Coward

I sit as still as life permits, watching you
sleep. True friend. What matters now? Love. Sleep. Talk.
Not to be inconsonant with your life,
or loiter death with long humiliations.
Flinching—as when a headlong train rushes
down on you like a bird of prey—I wait
for the beak in my shoulder; without you
I must learn to be a coward alone.

July: Colors

You touch me, consoling.
I hold one of your large hands that painted

24

violet storms and pink falling snow and
women the color of watermelon.
Now you wait for an idea to come,
to take you, to have the hot paint flow
like magma from your fingers; an idea
bigger than the Damoclean cancer,
to possess you, until it matters more
to paint than die.

July: Home

You come home in splendid summer, I bring
you a pink filipendula, too tall
to stand alone so I stake it, it leans
like an invalid in your garden.

August: Efflux

Friends visit—talking, burning all the candle
ends, reaching through residue to the raw bone
of love; surmounting. Each day more quicksand
passes through the glass until fever
of an unknown origin sets in. Your mouth
dries harder than a desert . . . only spray
as from a child's watering can fills
your eyes; its small amount, weightless in the sun.

September: Slippage

Monday your white hands freeze, hold on
to the guardrails, as though tossing
on the high seas. We all take turns sitting
on the bedside chair. Seesawing through
vacant rehearsals of hope, we are

the small figures you painted, waiting
through falling snow beside the gravestones,
in this, our first autumn without you.

Epilogue: 1

Your mother's father is standing on the wet
pier. I am standing beside him. He holds
his great hat, carefully, in his arm.
He is tall and very attractive.
He closes his eyes, then looks again
at this foreign harbor. I speak to him,

Epilogue: 2

"You will have two children here and die.
Your daughter will be given to a tailor,
but her daughter will paint the timeless
old ones. You will not know her, but I will
love her as though she were my child."

Clue

Did I give your hand away in my dream?
...someone woke me, someone I once knew—
and it was under *his* hand my eager breast
rose. His cupping hand, so desirous to stay,
rested there...but the body and the face
of the hand holding my breast was not
you. Swimming away hard from the dream
inside the dream, *I sensed that something*
was not right...
should I stay...touched by the
hand with an obscure face? and how
did I get under this loose blanket
in the first place? Awake, I hold
my breasts to search for clues; but who do I
look for, for both, for him, for you?

How to Know Your Ewe

for Jill Jakes

Is the woman crazy?
Blanche, the oldest sheep,
is lambing tonight and too old
to have a baby. Once
the woman wanted a baby.

Midnight: the barn is small
under cold stars. March glare-ice
stiffens the road; sheep bawl,
waiting for the woman.

><<

A metallic scum fills the barn,
the smell of body readiness:
Overcome, two maiden ewes
argue for the same small corner. . . .

Smell of silage in new wooden stalls,
in the pens of the mothers-to-be;
their swinging vulva doors loose and pink
as bubble gum—soon to pop a lamb or two.

Alone, she opens her book, "How to Know Your Ewe."

><<

"Giving up the law to raise sheep!"
She left the bench for sheep—judging them
a nobler service than the law.

The lamb is coming out backwards . . . *tail first* . . .
nose wiggles in pain . . . urgent bleating;
a volume of hot blood presses through—
as though a slaughter were taking place . . .
one leg is caught in the hot licorice dark.
Alarm: the woman's back curves almost
to a point, while one arm finds elbowroom
inside the ewe. Reaching deeper into
the womb she grabs the other leg, turning
the lamb in tender gore as though she
just opened her usual oven door. . . .

Tears of apology fall on the sore, mewing ewe
as the mountain slide of blood and lamb
finally divide.

><><

Abimelech, the great dog, died in her arms,
a wreath of flowers around his neck,
her passionate love words in his ear.
She named the next dog Justice, to ensure
there was some in the world; in her heart
she still longs for Justice.

><><

Animals live outside censure;
not creatures who seek beliefs,
they are scriptural mammals,
natural in their acts of grass and sky,
of standing still, of knowing when to die.

⋉⋊

The woman, exhausted from the birth,
cries out to see the lamb alive and black,
black as a judge's robes . . . hears the early
rain, soft and sane on the roof of the barn.

⋉⋊

Sheep and woman, modest bearers
of the long March light, rest together
among the sticky, glistening turds,
restored by the sanctity of afterbirth,
hands and hooves wrapped in the ooze of their doing.

Epilogue

There is the story of a princess
who would never remove her satin
slippers. One day a true prince asked her
to nakedly prove her love for him;
she refused; for under one slipper
she hid a small cleft hoof.

Tattoo

for Kaethe Weingarten

I

Three days and the edges of my iris brown
and tuck tight, the way you roll a handkerchief
hem. Remaining deep blue near the center
a hard yellow tongue licks up
its middle. Unlike the indigo iris
painted on French sugar cube wrappers...
unlike the periwinkle iris
in the border painting, "Tulips with Iris,"
from India's seventeenth-century Mugual...
mine are perishable, mortal...

II

unless tattooed onto a vertical *scar*
that can become the *stem* of an iris.
She said, "When the debriding is through,
sew my incision upright... I'll tattoo
an iris on its top, not the bearded kind—
but Siberian and blue." My friend,
a sheen of landscape: one perfectly rising
hill, one hand-made Serengeti fancy;
and in between, her lover does ex-
hilarate the changing scene.

III

On the verge of a detached retina,
replete with flashing lights and swampy

31

floaters, the doctor dilates my eyes.
Blinding white light produces second sight;
a filamental horror, roseate spider
webs pull me through space, lids jerk shut trying
to cry, but anesthesia prevents it.
He promises I am not going blind;
my aqueous fluid is sloshing off
a petal of skin with impunity—
diagnosis: aging.

IV

A bus stops for the light with a long
fart. My eye catches a woman with her back
pressed against a building. Winter swoops
her black fur through the gold hoops swinging
in her ears; she is lifting her face
to the sun, taking the small amount given,
imagining spring. A big yellow sun
is painted on the shopping bag
that hangs from her arm.

V

The skill of making life from loss
from cloth of any length or short
duration—from memory's bones we
become whole again: entice a paradise.

Clear Irresponsibility

Wooed to a rock in the clotted June green,
I sit, examining my family:
we map as we go, some retreating too slow

from the fray, as though saving face
were equivalent to grace (which means
standing your ground). In relief,

listening to chiming insects click-
ing their legs—I hear an interruptive
hissing in the weeds. Looking closer I see

an ovum, a dropped egg lying in
a grass heap; two feet further
a turtle in spasm, halfway

into a mud nest—weeping. Her weakened
hiss bends into long sighs as she cramps
down in her hot shell, fighting

to grip the birth site with her legs.
Straining, she gives up three slippery
grey eggs. Then, tamping the ground with her head,

she sleeps, withered from the effort. Gingerly,
I bend down to contemplate an irony
wreathing motherhood. Look at me

on my rock and she in her nest; neither
can resist the pull of parenthood.
I am recovering from a fight

with my daughter by hiding, soaking up summer,
heavy on my choking chest, till rest
seeps in and, eventually, pride returns.

Lifeless for twenty hard minutes,
she puffs out a rest; then her head makes a
three-quarter turn—assured her laid eggs

are hardening, she drags away,
leaving a trail of birth slime behind.
I envy her tough little self;

soon to have a cool frisk in the pond
while nature takes care of the rest.
Done with dispatch and no strings

attached. I envy her clear ir-
responsibility. No raising of babies
with plenty of lack of self-confidence.

Never ostracized for holding too close
or too long, and never to stand in the furrow
of apology, plowed in by self-doubt.

I enter the amniotic pond thinking
of her burrowing in this clay bowl
where my feet now stand, alien, in a hole.

Their Hippocampus Stomp

for Patricia

He asks her to dance and her square Hellenic
form hops up and down. Her hare lip arranges
itself into a moon-hanging smile and sticks
till he proposes.

She sees a fish leap from his pocket, rolls back
a milky eye and admits, *"I gu . . . esss so."* For forty
years she howls and shouts through every night;
his sleep is dreamless.

Now her front teeth are gone; she talks on the phone
holding her hand in front of her mouth.
For hours she sits alone on the sofa after chores
laughing at cartoons.

Afternoons they stroll in the park watching kids
play. *"Ina sunn where it's waarm . . . "* she sings.
Today she sees a docile bird with one black wing
whistling near her feet.

"It's a gi-rl! May-be we could a-dopt it. . . ." Barely
moving she checks his pocket for fish; holding
his breath he reaches deep into his pocket
and hands her a fish.

Omen for Women

1

Kneeling down under a grizzled sky
I see the loop is a snakeskin lying
in the road; beside it the squirted-out
insides are drying into a grey smear.
The skin has a ribbon-thin-look-careful
beauty: pricks of yellow flick both sides
of wavy blue and green lines, intricate
repetition of small design, a striking
grammar of form and space caught
in its cuneiform hurry to get across
a rush of summer highway.

Though we are not similar, snake, I am drawn
to the fact of your matter; you lacked
perspective and I the thrill of flashing
through gravity's grass. Your after-body
resembles a modern jewel: cruel silver head
blood gem-eye, tear-dropped tail . . . a jewel
with a yen to press warm flesh again?

2

When boys dared me I never had the nerve
to grab you by the tail and whirl you
around my head, throwing you as far as possible

like they did. And you, trying not to break
your spine, swerved your line, became black static
and snapped, scattering the air above my head,
eager to bracelet my arm and sting me,
sting me to death for all the imagined sins,
if you're male.

Come to think of it, so many times
             splitting your skin
you are a much better *omen for women*
             than the phallic fellows
who claim you. What if, regardless
             of your drape—*you are female?*
Half of us are . . . women of parts, always changing;
our only defense against oblivion.

                    3

So woman, you split your skin as you crossed
the road, raw and ready for new guises,
lovers, babies on the other side, heart made
to divide, increase, lose pieces; each time hoping
to be . . . *exactly* what is wanted. Were
you beached in confusion between one side
and the other or, as only we are,
between the beginning and the end;
baby half-in half-out, crying . . . when
is the moment the skin splits? Did you shout
out as I did, feet forked through cold stirrups,
oily sweat running into basins
between tits and mountain, bearing down cunt

muscle—"move—don't move—move—*DON'T MOVE . . .* "
the pain is the same—*the pain is the same*—
When is the moment *THE SKIN SPLITS OFF?*

The moment you halved me to plant a pit—
old skin and lives split and dropped away,
the moment I exploded to come with you
leaving all others behind—that
was the moment the skin came off. . . .

4

AH NOW! water's running down my legs,
        laughing, high as a kite,
wet seaweed hair, knees red from bites,
        this is the moment the skin comes off! "PUSH."
A sudden widening inside . . .
        PUSH!
a shoulder ripples out, an arm is attached,
        elbows flap up . . .
knees washboarding through . . .

and I collapse like a squeezed tomato
covering you, my lover, with birth blood—
covering the ardent aftereffects
of our laying act. You hardening
and erect at my side renewing me so
I would do it again with my splitting
miracle skin, in sickness and in soreness
right here right now on this sacred, public,
slimy, lovesick gurney.

5

Omen for Women, now I see our
resemblance. Holding up your skin I ask,
"For whom is the message of your scribble
line across the textual, hot summer asphalt?"

The One That Got Away

O h h h ... Gulliver ... what ever happened to the *old* story?
    tangled silken threads, *the humiliating story,*
holds me down to a steel hotbed
      scanning scanning ...
puts a cup of chalk in my hand marked
      DRINK
while the machine-hawk angles
      into position
eyeballs my subterranean system
      and drops rays like rocks
too close inside my cockeyed mind ...

chalky dogwoods petticoating Kentucky hills
    talking ... in the middle of a sermon
      in the middle of a stream
a baptism in Appalachia
  two guys from Cincinnati in madras jackets
drop grandma in the stream where she floats
      akimbo—

an old minnow of a gal who finally survives to meet her Maker
    preacher-man—hand on his meaty cheek
billows it out till hy-per-VEN-til-ATION pumps up
      the airways to God, resurrects our throaty nods
and incomprehensible words ... detach ...
      fly up alone till we are singing, yawning and crying
"Save me Now, I am reborn ... !"

while the machine attached to me

is molded to my shape—
the custom cold steel holds me,
   a spread-eagle Gulliver
in place for my two-minute zap....
   they are not concerned with the ending
or whether my form is too short or too long...
      in this time
I go back to the coal mine,
   it falls in every week
and the women, red-eyed,
   tear up the street
yelling, *"doctor, doctor, where's the..."*

(my father,) *"My GOD, are you here again!"*
goes down to the mine while I
hide under the dining room table
till they release me, help me off,
and I apply my clothes
like bandages.

to be continued...

Three

Kinshit

It's summer: none of the toilets will flush;
just enough water for a half-swirl wets
the sides, coughs, and stops. No more dependable
inrush, no more effective outrush. Toilets
sweating like mad; bowl—cold as a handshake
that marks your skirt when you wipe it off.
And the toilet paper buildup on top
is like rotten cabbage, breaking up
in the pot. Conjuring, we get the snake,
a metal catheter, and force it in
to pull out the backed-up slab . . .
nothing. Next the plunger hiccups the waters—
pureeing its contents, but—no flush occurs!

Just the foul floats of summer, still floating.
For the next two days Draino reigns, and four drums
later, we resort to a *case* of lemon
air freshener till the air stinks with the scent
of lemon shit. Something is running amok
inside our septic tank and no fool stools
are to blame. We wake at 3:00 a.m.
to gassy tank noises; jiggle the handle
in a useless ritual, watching our mini
galaxies not go down! With each pseudo-flush
it seems more strangers appear, orbiting
what has to be yours and mine—who are they?
are they *our own*? reproducing? breaking up?

The children caught in our shit again?
Intrusive mother, accusing child:
and even you (at times), the stale mate!
No margin of error here for shit
to happen—Whodunit? me I guess,
the usual culprit. But, I argue, shit
is the witty insurer of familiar-
ity; our circuitry that stays! We lean
over the bowl, the nebula-like tea leaves—
or heavenly bodies, as though we were out
on the hill for our nightly count of
sanitary stars, reflecting on
the creation myths of kith and kinshit.

Birdy

Everyone thought it a strange name, for a cat, "Bird," but it suited her. A luminous white cat with chickadee grey bangs hanging into her eyes that seemed outlined in kohl. A proper predatory domestic, she dropped creatures who didn't survive the cruel hunt carefully into her bowl. Mornings I would find a small, silky gallbladder, like an iridescent green and purple lapillus, glued like a jewel to the middle of the porch. Spring was her favorite season; she loved to sing in the garden, accompanying me while I hauled rocks and placed out the flowers.

The bitter winter day she disappeared, we had seen eagles flying in the woods and feared their spurs had hooked her Venus coat, carrying her to a hidden perch to despoil and consume her; high drama for an old lazy girl who ran the meadows and drank from cold streams and once, in one of her nine lives, leapt straight off the porch, three stories high and landed on all fours, as tradition has it.

The barn was always her home away from home; slatted light and a ripe smell made a perfect birth place for her two kittens. After three days, she carried them in her mouth through the house, placing them under the guest room beds.

I guessed she might be in the barn but had to quickly turn away to avoid the view of her backside, eaten off by the haggard runner, the winter coyote. We could hear their wavering bark at night but thought them far away.

We wrapped her in her blanket, filling it with dried winter flowers and my still blooming pink house geranium, so that she could enter the days ahead with the appropriate symbols of her house and her attendants. Egyptian kings notice those who arrive with gifts of love.

Her opus over, I wish to tell her one more story: there is a small, fat song bird from California, who mews like a cat when fighting for its survival; she would have appreciated the irony.

When we found her she was lying in her favorite position: on her side, feet outstretched and tail up in a long perfect curve. Very close to my favorite position when I am on my side and you are curled around me from behind, with your arm slung over my middle, one knee under my seat and your fur tickling my back.

matters of the flesh

for Molly and Yann

alight

flesh of my flesh
you travel so fast
down the hall
down the hospital hall
your gown rushes out
like angel wings

angel

one hand wheeling your pole
tubes running out of you
through bags dripping
back into you

in another circulation
you were attached to me ...
here is your second boy

you look awful

the new one quiet as a melon
sleeps flaunting a raspberry navel

while you my daughter run down the hall
keeping your first son's hand
espaliered to your side,
his apple eyes ripening in yours
(so dark and swollen from pushing)

to a quiet corner in the solarium . . .
talking with your two-year-old boy
giving him wrapped presents
from the new baby
his small back so very straight
as he listens to his new story
trying to size himself to the day.

together

I can see this love as though
it were matter, it rises as steam rises up
from deep hot springs
can you see it
there there oh there

love

somewhere between the strawberry
jam on his finger
and his plastic bib of strawberries
a vapor surrounds you

the spirit

weeping his visit over he must leave
his face breaks
with the weight of his new destiny
such a small boy his song
disappearing with the elevator

she is my matter
these are hers

matter

through flesh
around flesh
holding onto flesh
coming through flesh
we are housed

double and triple ourselves
in human mathematics
the rockabye of toothpick bones

not hair
not sight
not words
not sounds
not yet
firefly life on off on off

Phantoms

I have been carrying
my leg for sometime now.
Hopping forward is slow
progress; one elbow
hangs by a thread and
must rest on my dead hip.
I had to leave my head behind
sometime ago; it thoughtlessly
banged against the rocks. Now I'm
afraid my other leg will fail
from this plague of constant
movement—then I'll have to
pull forward on one elbow and
one shoulder. There! I hear its
brittle cracking off; it falls.
Now all my limbs are gone.
Lacking limbs, my navel
snails across the ground,
inching along on its
own moisture; it
grips, then slips my
heavy torso forward,
spitting out the dust,
gasping with every
step. I am going
to a small sphere
where there
is no pain.
I can

crawl in
almost tight.
No daylight.
One leg used
to stick out—
Now it won't,
of course.
Once there,
I keep
my eyes
closed;
remembering
walking
and swinging
my high school
hips.

Eye Lines

Hovering like a humming bird in the five-and-
dime, this time with money to buy, colors
from far bazaars—eyeliners to draw in
my immaterial self that might draw
glances back... I catch my jelly-fish face
bobbing in the tinted mirror; scared
at its own aphrodisiac wish. Will I
look like a stained glass window? *A dead
saint poured red and blue between leaded lines?*

I watch my hand roll over the containers,
searching for the right one: the color
with hidden instructions, like a thief
trying to pinch an image. Then suddenly
I see it, *"Opalescent"* powder!
"Opalescent!" I love the name so much
I would change mine on the spot. Furtively,
I screw out a matching lip shade, *"Red Hot Red."*

The only colors I've been able
to collect are the occasional bruises
of abuse—(as though they are acceptable
blueprints for a person). But *now*
is the outlined time to approach the world...
fourteen and hormones shaking like our old
furnace my father swore would explode
someday and send us all to kingdom come.

My mother couldn't fill me in about boys:
my mother-of-pearl mother couldn't
blush my lips or line my eyes with turquoise;
together we are thin slices of kiwi
drifting on a wave. Her powder is "matte,"
which flattens her face like a plate.
Being fair she feels it covers the faint
bouquets of roses in her cheeks. Like snow
that doesn't really fall, I flurry
to the street, the ransom of transformation
under my arm. Soon to be made visible
in my lustrous moon powder, I go home.

Holding up the mirror, I see my mother's
face waving toward me from the door: her clinking
glass, a lighthouse on the rocks. In sober days
she said: "Do something they'll remember!"
She eyes my spoils: *"Oh makeup! Did you bring some
for me?"* I put down my mirror, she puts down
her glass, smiling like a child as I make her up.

Drawing in face-saving lines, I restore
her planes with gypsy blue and coral rouge;
then weave a braid of basil leaves to rest
upon her chest. So bandaged in sweet greens,
she swims toward me in the foam; her shining
scales reflecting, catch me to her breast;
the waves between us bearing the unbearable—

Rackety Songs

Near a small reflecting pond, newly made
and far to the right of the wedding lawn,
a weeping larch, grown on its mown edge,
bows her head in a long curve, aware
of the fair blue heron's dawn approach.
Astir, his neck arches down in degree of curve,
like the larch, producing the thought
of a heart between them. Wrought so fast
as to practice her stillness, the heron
steps invisibly forward; softly
the larch cries out, wet with dew
(and don't), leans her belly needles closer
not to lose his scent, and feels
his moving wind, sweet with sin

when, scanning for crayfish, his head's
slightest turn follows her unspoken wish
for approach. The shape is nearly drawn,
their beaks will touch and soft lines of arms
be once and only around each other,
then gone. When something in the wind, unfinished,
moves them closer... he crosses behind her...
and passing, they cut figure eights as on ice.
Winds sigh for the passing of unlasting
hearts and a small commotion of birds
sing rackety songs of fidelity. The heron
fishes in his own reflection, long
beyond the larch, as a watching tree drops
its tattered leaves, fainting to the ground.

Double Date

Sitting sideways, wearing only boxer shorts,
he waits up for me long after midnight:
reading the newspaper between naps,
sipping beer from "ponies," he says,
"to ride out the night," repeatedly
restubbing out his cigarettes . . . so afraid
of fire. Parked in a pale green Chevy
on the street above the house we see
him in the window; my father, walking
back and forth from the fridge to his chair.

Occasionally, he lingers in the window,
pulls out the elastic band of his shorts—
lets it snap back and, looking as though
he can see us, he stares, it seems, directly
at me. Me—unbuttoning my blouse
on the street above our house, in love
with a boy who marries a girl who looks
like me; trading hickeys in the dark
until we are as red as the backsides
of those bluenosed monkeys we see

in the National Geographic. After
midnight, I thumb the latch on the door,
trying to sneak past the snores, but he hears,
looks at his watch, rubs his crew cut and pulls
a cigarette into his disappearing lips.
He wakes to tell me the story of his life.

Snared by the heat of his reddening neck
and the tension in his bare, cupped-up toes,

I listen to his old story through
belches and smokes: the Monongahela
River bridge, dawn, shoes in hand, feet scorched
from shoveling iron ore down the blast furnaces—
putting himself through medical school.
Tears fall down his red brick flesh.
Suffocating in malt, I intermittently
drop my head so he won't see me
burn—hot with excitement at his pain.
Profane words like pinballs, collide, buck . . . recoil—

as the tantrum of his naked history
sticks again in my throat. He chokes on a swig
of beer and pushes the face of his cigarette
into the ashtray till it crumbles.
Long after midnight, I sit alone in
my window, confused by a night of wooing.
I cup my erect nipples to make them
soft and pray for the green Chevrolet to slip
back, parked and humming for me in the dark.

Vets

Dimes in metal taps c l i c k to Gene Krupa's sticks...
hup! we're in the forties in sil-ver shoes and heels—
bul-lets tap so fast we hear our own kriegspiel.

Brush-stamp-heel-toe, learning how to jive,
we're tapping our hearts out, trying to stay alive!
Fol-lowing the se-quins, we wing flap a path,
air-plane foot-lights *flash* before the *crash*....

Star flags hang in windows for the boys *OVER
THERE*; silver, means he's missin', blue, he's still alive,
gold he is a goner and every-body cries!

Daddy-O is home from war and both redheads,
mom and I are chanting, "He's alive, not dead!"
Throwing me a boozy smile, he smokes his Lucky Greens—
hands shake from drinking, my mother snipes, "Obscene"

> *(Song) I came here to talk for Joe,*
> *He wants me to let you know,*
> *that he can't keep that date with you*
> *toniiightt....*

Dad Drops his duffel bag and grabs my dancin' hand,
I shuffle off to Buffalo around my ribboned man,
Oh we will live forever, and we will all be free—
bars are shining on his sleeve, walkin' down the street with me.

...until he gets the bends. His gut continues
bleeding and his marriage doesn't mend.
At night he holds my baby brother
—calls him GI Joe—they slow dance in the
the livin' room, he's humming really low.

Women had affairs but rarely wrote them down;
they said they had "amnesia," and wandered out of town.
They penned sweet thoughts to absent boys, "to keep
the men alive"...then every single spring
my mom broke out in hives.

> *(Song) Fly the ocean in a silver plane...*
> *see the jungle when it's wet with rain...*
> *just remember to come home again...*
> *you belong to me....*

He taught me how to dance, rehearsing
my first date. Cowering—I watch him
submitting to his fate; he moves to the couch
where he smokes and masturbates.

Pomade in his hair and hard as a pear,
a sallow boy named Lowell presses against
me to the beat of *Temptation* and we tease

the future slow dancing between our legs....
My saddle shoes leap to follow his spins,
my nervy, navy pleats jump clear of his shoulder,

back flips, hip hits, we jitterbug our brains out;
front seat acrobats in *pseudo*-sexual stunts—
armpits smells *forever* on my white Angora sweater!

One day in Algebra two vets arrive;
it's like a visitation to have these men alive.
Hands like torn roots, hanging down their sides.

Seeds and friends are scattered in *European theaters* . . .
what do you say at fourteen to grown up men??

—Clark bar man
don't bar me
from your heart—
this mallow, shallow
wrapper girl
who licks a candy paper moon
hangin' in the milky way—
is gift wrapped for a kidnap.
if you don't have the clap—

Flipping their zippos
we snub them like hoboes.
Thrilled with the popsicle sticks
we lick in front of boys—
(our communication toys)—
words on the tongue run
up the rung of their eyes
woe hobo whoa—
Hey bucking bronco; flinch-
ing at a shadow?

"Did you ever see a dildo??"
"Shut up Dorothea . . . he's gonna cry."
"Can't he yell, TAKE IT OFF?"
It's a Goddamn peep show in Steubenville,
Ohio for Chrissake!
Ohhhh what a creep!

Hey nothin went off—relax, you're back!"

> *(Song) My heart is sad and lonely*
> *for you I cry, for you dear only . . .*
> *why can't you believe me*
> *I'm all for you . . . body and soul.*

We whisper:
. . . are they *experienced?*
. . . *how many times* did they . . . ?
. . . weren't they in . . . *Paris??*
. . . Shouldn't we be patriotic—
. . . even merciful, and just *give it to them?*
Eyes shining like olives
stinging with tears,
we spread our legs . . . *FOR THE WAR!*
clasp them tight . . . *FOR THE WAR!*
remote boys who dropped bombs *FOR THE WAR!*
weep on top of us *FOR THE WAR!*
shuddering your grateful shoulders,
huge elephant noises in your throats
till your trunks goes up   up   up!
FOR THE WAR!

$\times\!\times$

They had *two* military funerals,
one for each boy who died. Suicide...?
We all walk behind the drums in time
arummmm—step—arumm—step—arumm—
Guns click—BABANG—click—click—BABANG....
Everyone waiting in the long silence,
some try to understand, some just wait.

One vet chewed a pencil he kept behind his ear,
I thought he would die of lead poisoning—
but he died of alcoholism like my father.
Was the pencil there when he drove that heap

off the cliff, playing chicken war
with the brother of his buddy who was
killed in action? I hardly knew the other guy;
he didn't finish out the year, grew a beard
and walked out.

They set aside a plot and buried them
next to each other in a remote part
of the cemetery. No one could figure
if their plot was allowed inside the boundaries
or out—but proximity seemed to bring
them closer to us. Rain made the earth
soft that day, almost invitational.
Our feet made sucking sounds, like gasping,
as we walked behind the two families;
strangers whose sons had survived the war.
Like small dark birds, they disappeared over the hill.

(Song) For it's a long long time from May to December...
and the days grow short... when you reach September...

His Christmas present—a purple satin tie
with a hand-painted St. Bernard on it.
I have fallen in love with a navy vet
who calls me "His suburban Modigliani."
Stretched out almost naked on his small bed
we are discussing Ralph Waldo Emerson
and the size and shape of my breasts.
A few sequins from my old white sweater
fall from time to time, sticking to us.

Four

So Close

"No intimacies for now," the doctor says.
You ask me, *"Will this time be too long for you,*
too hard?" Imperceptibly a callus grows
on our desire—but amenities
prevail and though sodden with longing,
we behave indifferent here, incurious there.
Helpfully, our pruned hearts shrivel; and weather
stays untroubled, grey. Leaning over
you at night, breathing in our shared breath,
helps my parachuting lungs resist
their clattering fall, and limb from limb
they fold their ride along your shapely side.
In dreams we lie becalmed . . . and wait to catch
each other's tide. I shift my bosom
to where you feel it most; remembrance
held within the distance—". . . too hard for me,"
I say, "when we've become so close?"

same old ground

leaves ride flashing briefly in the sun
rondos blow falling turning tips up come
down golden singles perform *down*
twos flirt softly *down*
a sudden rain of leaves lets
go bedding *down* the earth
two solo strangers from ash and oak
in slowed free fall touch *down*
(some wish to do it again
flamenco-style heros crush to get
down first to catch someone)
some fall *down* at night
ashamed they couldn't hold on
today at the fair you felt dizzy as a leaf
"I need to lie down" you breathed
"the two I love best are those that fall together"
and I flutter *down* to sleep alongside you

Billet Deux

Today you're leaving for Africa; thank God
it's after I've had the colonoscopy...
and he tells me I have a redundant colon—

I say, who needs a gastrointestinal
editor? Running out I tear my damn
thigh muscle! Listen, I fall down too much,

and *where are you* ...! (She hobbles on her crutch
to the fridge.) I'll host a meal! Invite my friends,
heal.... Take out a bird to roast...wash cavity,

pull out innards...lemon juice...garlic rub...
what's *that*? TWO HEARTS? two hearts! My God, *two hearts*!
What does this mean, is it a spare part

so that if one falters, the other receives
the torch, and—runs on? (laughter) With you missing
I'm too vulnerable to metaphors like:

these forevermore hearts lie in my hand ...
while a sharp knife hesitates in the other....
Perfect little koans, pint-size drummers—

like my grandfather's watch that I loved.
Perhaps the extra is like his pocket heart
chiming when he checked his time. What's the oath

that locked them close together, so they stayed
alive? Could a Siamese song have flowed through both—
like, *"You are my heart,"* like, *"You are my heart"*?

Surgery

Sniffing my stockings I am reminded
of the French waiter who loved the hat check girl
because of the smell of her stockings ...

it is the crossing of mind and leg that emanates.
In the hospital the smell of solution
defoliates the institution,

staying high in my nostrils.
Clothes, unfleshed, fall in small heaps,
follow me to the bathroom, I weep.

Tattooed tears never come off.
Listen, water swishes in the sink—
white Woolite maidens gather to purify

their subjects. Wiping out the day, I lie
on the bathroom floor, coiled around every thought.
I am cold, there is a strong smell

of oleander. Looking up I see
my soul standing on a chair, wavering
there like a necessary thing. . . .

"I thought I gave you away," I shout.
She hunches her shoulders, frightened at my tone,
then offers, "I'm not very good at relationships. . . ."

Words appear as though
in air

you nearly died! she cries.

Postcard

Amsterdam: folded in these Dutch geometries,
I sip my Bengal tea. Blossoms so dry
a minute ago, steep and stretch and float.
Musk and bay oil spice the small café where
I write; I am writing the word *distance*—
to see how far I can go—
even traveling, my mind still wanders
back—past borders harboring exotica
where ships have come and gone to Jakarta—
where they wear hats to keep their souls from
flying out. If you were to fly in again,
hatless, I would tie the world about my waist—
my train stretching everywhere to catch your
feathers, dry leaves, even stones. Will you feel
me when this Dutch blue card touches your hand?

Ordinarily Your Nose

Flies are the real nosologists;
they land on your nose,
count their legs as they look up
your nose at you and make
a diagnosis: tasty or no?

While you, my great chorister, doze:
your honking membrane,
inhales like a taut sail, and
snaps out its hankerings
and fleshy lamentations.

Or, closes around mine
in a Picasso, nose-closing kiss—
juxtaposing our angles
to prevent vertigo
as we fall asprawl on our asses;
our gecko fingers
sucking hard on the glass.

Ordinarily your nose can sniff me
out in the dark—
a weather vane whiff
finds freshets for love
finds the vulva plum
to lie on your tongue,
finds saliva gathering like lace
around a Valentine....

And after love

You sneeze so violently
we inch up toward the Kleenex box
hoping to keep our clinch
laughing our heads off.
When the fly returns, unabashed,
she lands between your nose
and eyelash; the diagnosis
has changed: tasty.

Drought

The week you leave, the drought is record high:
water lilies crawl to shore, gagging
on the pale mud, their luminous centers
closed. Black pansies crisp in this fire;
I think of snow and close the windows.
Opposites attract, as we did. I weigh
my bosoms in my hands, and even they
seem stale balloons. Perhaps constancy
is too hard to bear, or age prepares
us badly for surprise. Or, in the hot
doubt of rage, love dries; folds its tent against
the storm and womb-like waits for it to pass.
Why are you surprised? This is how we last.

Hyacinth

Stately upright stalk! Swaying from the weight
of sheer empurplement. Hyacinth, savored bloom,
opening and disclosing till the sudden
drop date stretches the swooning neck
over the pot rim; as a child's head rolls
round the bosom, imparting its sweet mauve power.
I yearn to eat this giddy, crunchy scent,
this bloom of satin parts folded left
to right, then right to left in dizzying
ambivalence. I rub the blossoms cross
my lips and each one breathes back on me from
tiny throat pipes that swell to my touch.
Secret lavender skin, limp from too much
rapture; this quick flower of love sanctifies
a fever too strong for a love time so brief;
wilting in my hand, dying in its grief.

The Day Before His Marriage

for Matt and Candace

Folding his arms
at the water's edge,
his feet bury deeper
with every provocation
of the waves. Eyes are
skyward gathering blue,
I watch the water hit and miss us
with its jeweled light.
Small and laughing,
I hold him by the scruff
of his puppy neck,
and he runs toward the water
trying to catch it whole.

Later
when there was a stone on his heart, I could
feel it on mine as though a pendulum
swung between us, unmoved by time, and the arc
of separation narrowed to the time
his heartbeat lay under mine. He turns, I wave,
smiling from my distance as though to say,
what are you doing...just s t a n d i n g out there?
He smiles back, skips his stone expertly
across the water; dives after it and swims—
racing in his boy's crawl to manhood; now
sweetened with the certainty of what's beneath,
and what's above; certainty of lover
and of love.

L'arrangement: Paris

for Biala and Alain

A still French lily sits in the lavender window. Its cloudy blue center resembles the motionless eyes of the tall quiet man she loves. His fingers hang like tubes of color against a canvas apron. He knows each of her small flower paintings by heart and arranges them one by one, in the light as he feels it coming from the window; such a good color check. When she returns they will decide which of her paintings will hang in the small gallery.

><

The vase clasps dim, pink
tulips swooning recklessly
over the balcony rim;
young girls watching the parade
from their vase—hoping to meet
soldiers, crossing and uncrossing
their pale citron stems.

><

...this one in the drawer of her writing table...

><

Bosomy white peonies
kiss the clamorous red amaryllis
to teach it tact. An almond
blossom, blind to its own fact,
almost opens before its time.

79

><

... another in the seat of the chair where he sleeps ...

><

Midst the ruby saliva, one
love lies bleeding, droops ...
two infallibly blue dahlias meet
in the belly of a white pitcher
with curved Japanese feet.

><

Two 18th-century metal gates protect their quiet street. He hears them
open and close; the sound is harsh but protective. They are alone: she
is ninety-two, he is ninety-four. Outside, she is painting a canvas the
size of a wall; a bird feeder filled with birds, all lightly dusted in snow.

... He leans her favorite against the small fireplace ...

><

Six plum and white anemones stand
in a grey jar crossed with bars of sand
on stripes of a blue and white
table cloth in her kitchen, beside
two fowl, parsley and a casserole.

><

Small green birds came this winter, like pieces of darkness flying up
and up through the snow; hearing their pattern of flight, he smiles at

the competition of the chatterpin noisters. Standing in an open doorway, he hears her brush slide and touch the paper; color threads through his eyes like fire in Mexican opals.

$$\times\!\!\times$$

He raps on the window, goes to the fridge and feels for lunch, another day, it's time for their break.

Once in a Blue Moon

I still recognize myself once in a blue moon
—the way cows looking over their shoulders, sense
a hurricane laboring inland and swoon.

Our particular hurricanes used to come
in the afternoon; now an occasional typhoon
blows by us—but a hurricane? oh, maybe

once in a blue moon. Sheets like candy twists
strewing our bed; parachuting through
tree spaces, we fall limb from limb,

singing "Blue Moon" with Mel Torme...
some time ago, before the sooty glance
of age fell on our resemblances.

Smudged, we sit like two old grave rubbings
and you have to guess what excited
our crooning bodies once in a blue moon.

Beneath this elusive blue moon, we dream...
but our suppliant faces have no power
in distance; whereas *she*, serene, bends

the tree's evening shadows to their velvet knees.
Sometimes I know you don't quite see me—
but then I recognize myself in you—
and that's only...once in a blue moon.

Have-a-Heart

He shoots up onto the porch, two stories high,
stares a lugubrious stare at us
through the glass kitchen door; Halloween
trickster, disappointed there's no cat food
left in the outside bowls. As I take the broom
he cocks a rakish head and disappears
over the side on a ladder of air.
He wins every time; feeding his wife,
family, lover, who knows, the neighborhood.
Each morning I find a semaphore of dirt
from his repast which spells "Up Yours" to my broom

and me. We manage to catch the raccoon
in our "Have-a-Heart Trap." He looks out at us,
lofty, in his raccoon reproach. At the top
of the neighboring hill, before we spring
the trap I say, *"When I open this trap, run!*
Remember, captive fear is the call to action. . . ."
As I see him tear away down the hill,
mask darting through the high oat grass,
I feel humiliated by our steel and wire cage,
out of bounds, I say to myself.

First dream: The raccoon and I are on a raft
sailing down a peaceful river and he catches
a fish—I presume for us—but the fish is
alive as he takes his first bite. This
partnership is harder than I think.

Second dream: I am pushing him into
a small oven but can't get him all in—
his fur persists in sticking out
all around the chrome frame—
his elbow, as strong as mine, keeps the door
wedged open. It is equal war.

><

After the dreams under a cold moon,
he comes again. Gloomily, he lumbers
across the porch seeming somehow wistful.
Twice, he checks the empty bowl. The cats
see him and hissing, throw themselves against
the window, cartoon-style. He is older than I
thought, and, I recognize, a little arthritic
in his hips. Standing inside with my broom,
I watch him crawl into the cats' outdoor bed;
he looks back at me as though to ask,
Can he flop here for the night? He's been in
some fights; several patches of skin show through
his thinner back fur. He scratches on the window;
looking at his dark fleshy palm I think,
only a hand away from the primordial mud.

Everything Comes

for Ethan, Dylan, Liam, and Aidan

When we first dig the pond
I want to plant sedge
you say, wait, the birds
will bring it on their feet.
I cheat and plant "Meadow in a Can,"
because I can't wait.

November: neighbors are laughing, we have made
this *crater*! Is this your *battleground*
they ask—abort the whole pond thing!
I wear a path around its winter edge,
howling into the big mud mouth,
protesting emptiness.

$\times\!\times$

You are the believer it will fill
as surely as you sit in the church pew
thigh to thigh with me. In winter
we argue by phone; you are leaving me
with a big raw hole in the ground,
its bald roots, scarified: wonky
nerve ends unable to find comfort
under the snow—too cold, too sad to grow.

$\times\!\times$

Spring: the dogwood's white cups
pink up, shivering in excitement . . .

85

so *neon green* is your return.
Together we pull out and burn
the duckweed slowly choking
the throat of our muddy puddle—
surely! it is *water* trickling in . . . !
Climbing red columbine intertwines
with sedge; bonfires light
the pond with small red flames,
they celebrate the baby, they make us tame.

Three more Springs:
the second baby sleeps
from room to room. We fret
about a distant friend
who hasn't called.
We practice sleeping
in the afternoon,
young Mozart's music
travels through the air.
Time is plain . . .
each drop of day hangs
heavily . . . lambs bleat for grain,
it's only four o'clock again. . . .

><

Even in a pond an undertow exists;
one day a line plays
through your familiar face
and stays: age, making us new.

><

Winters come with elegies:
Sister, father, two mothers,
then, our oldest friend . . .
Bare branches shake
in the breaking storms—crack off.
A bloody red euonymus,
growing on the edge of the pond,
doesn't, damn it, die.

×—×

Thirty years:
two truckloads of white sand
make their summer beach,
the size of a postage stamp.
Down the hill rolls a troupe
of little boys; four hoops of light
falling in feather towel-capes
ready to do their rain dance
in the rain . . . nothing less
than enchantment, I chant.

×—×

Floating beyond the middle
of the pond, already feeling
the coolness of night,
water up to my ears,
eyes on the sky,
I wait for your dive,
knowing it will come,
everything comes.

may evening

some of us trim
the lawn
some of us look
for our wallet
some of us wipe
the dishes
some of us
walk the dog
some of us
have a bone scan
some of us yawn
and check our watches
some of us
have radiation
for the second time

in the cities
may blossoms fall
on concrete sidewalks
wondering
what's the next step

on a day I remember
warm then as now
a day like body temperature

a forlorn wind
stirred the leaves
buds still tight
and white green

I heard a car door

slam
they are going somewhere
without me
a punishment

I am going
somewhere too
sitting in my window
and never coming back.

Acknowledgments

✕✕

"Dancing in the Dark"—*Paris Review* #131
"The Soup"—*Paris Review* #131
"Polity"—*Beloit Poetry Journal*, Summer 1993
"Zona Viva"—*Beloit Poetry Journal*, Summer 1993
"Phantoms"—*Beloit Poetry Journal*, Summer 1993
"Open"—*Western Humanities Review*, July 1996
"the one that got away"—*Western Humanities Review*, July 1996
"Omen for Women"—*Southern Poetry Review*, Winter 1997
"Kinshit"—*Paris Review* #147
"Torment"—*e: The 1998 Emily Dickinson Award Anthology 1999*
"Matters of the Flesh"—*New Millennium*, June 2000
"Eye Lines"—*Kimera*, June 2000

Special thanks
to Molly Peacock, Richard Howard, Elise Paschen,
and my publisher, Joan Cusack Handler,
for their unwavering support of my work.